AI for Personal Tax Preparation

Smart Solutions for Stress-Free Tax Filing

By Joe Correa

Published by Live Stronger Faster

This book is for educational and informational purposes only. The author and publisher are not engaged in rendering legal, financial, tax, or other professional advice. Readers should consult a qualified professional before making any financial decisions.

First Edition

Table of Contents

Introduction

For most people, taxes have always been one of life's most stressful, confusing, and financially dangerous obligations. Every year, millions of individuals—employees, freelancers, investors, retirees, and business owners—face the same ritual of gathering documents, guessing what qualifies as a deduction, worrying about mistakes, and hoping they don't receive a dreaded IRS letter months later. Despite living in the most technologically advanced era in human history, the tax system has remained stubbornly complex, fragmented, and intimidating. But that era is now ending. Artificial intelligence is transforming personal tax preparation in ways that were unimaginable just a decade ago, replacing anxiety, inefficiency, and human error with precision, automation, and real-time intelligence.

This book exists because the tax world has quietly crossed a technological tipping point. AI tax software no longer just fills out forms—it understands your financial life. Modern tax engines analyze your income streams, investment activity, banking transactions, expenses, property records, and prior filings in seconds. They recognize patterns, spot inconsistencies, and optimize every line of your return. Where human preparers once relied on checklists and experience, AI relies on massive data models trained on millions of real tax outcomes. The result is a system that does not guess—it calculates. It does not forget—it remembers everything. It does not overlook—it cross-checks. This changes what it means to file taxes.

For the first time in history, individual taxpayers have access to the same class of technology that governments, banks, hedge funds, and multinational corporations use to manage financial risk and compliance. What was once available only to billion-dollar enterprises is now accessible on your phone. AI tax preparation platforms can import your W-2s, 1099s, brokerage statements, crypto wallets, rental income, and business transactions automatically. They can identify missing forms, flag discrepancies, and simulate multiple filing strategies to determine which one legally produces the lowest tax bill. This is not incremental improvement—it is a fundamental redesign of how taxes are prepared.

The old model of tax filing was built for paper. It was built for manual entry, slow processing, and delayed feedback. You filled out forms, mailed them, waited weeks or months, and hoped everything was correct. Even when digital filing arrived, it mostly replicated the same logic on a screen. You still had to know what to enter. You still had to find the numbers. You still had to hope nothing was missed. AI eliminates that entire workflow. It ingests data directly from financial institutions, employers, payroll systems, and investment platforms. It verifies identity, validates transactions, reconciles totals, and checks compliance automatically. The human is no longer doing the calculations—the human is simply approving them.

This shift is especially powerful because personal finance has become more complex than ever. People no longer have just one employer and one W-2. They have gig income, rental income, digital products, crypto trades, stock options, side hustles, online businesses, and global payments. Traditional tax software struggles with this complexity because it relies on static rules and rigid workflows. AI systems thrive in complexity. They were built to analyze large, messy, constantly changing datasets. That makes them perfectly suited for modern financial lives. Whether you earn money on Uber, Airbnb, YouTube, Etsy, real estate, or crypto exchanges, AI can track it, classify it, and apply the correct tax treatment automatically.

Another revolutionary change is accuracy. Human tax preparers make mistakes. Even highly trained professionals are limited by fatigue, time pressure, and incomplete information. AI does not suffer from any of these constraints. It runs validation checks across every line of the return. It compares your filing to millions of similar taxpayers to identify anomalies. It cross-references IRS rules, state regulations, and local tax codes in real time. If something looks off, it flags it. If something could be optimized, it models it. This dramatically reduces both underpayment and overpayment of taxes. You no longer have to worry that you left money on the table or that you accidentally triggered an audit.

Speed is another transformation. What used to take hours, days, or weeks now takes minutes. A fully automated AI tax platform can assemble a complete return in the time it takes to make a cup of coffee. That speed is not just convenient—it is strategic. It allows you to run "what-if" scenarios instantly. You can see how different deductions, filing statuses, investment moves, or income changes would affect your taxes before the year even ends. Tax filing becomes tax forecasting. Instead of reacting to what happened last year, you can proactively shape what happens next year.

This book will show you how this new world works from the inside. You will learn how AI tax engines ingest data, how they classify income and expenses, how they interpret IRS rules, and how they produce accurate filings at machine speed. You will understand the difference between rule-based software and machine-learning systems, and why the latter is dramatically more powerful. You will see how AI spots deductions, prevents errors, and protects you from compliance risks. Most importantly, you will learn how to use these tools to take control of your financial life.

For taxpayers, this is not just about convenience—it is about power. Knowledge asymmetry has always been the hidden tax. Governments and large institutions have always had better data, better models, and better tools than individuals. AI flips that dynamic. It gives everyday people access to the same analytical firepower that the IRS uses to detect fraud and enforce compliance. When you use AI for tax preparation, you are no longer guessing—you are operating with precision.

This matters because taxes are not just an annual chore. They are one of the largest financial forces in your life. Over a lifetime, most people will pay more in taxes than they will spend on housing, education, or healthcare. A small improvement in tax efficiency compounds into massive wealth over time. AI makes that efficiency accessible. It turns tax preparation from a once-a-year headache into an always-on optimization engine.

As you move through this book and the rest of the series, you will begin to see your taxes not as something to fear, but as something to engineer. You will understand how your income flows, how your expenses interact, how deductions are calculated, and how filing strategies are optimized. You will see how artificial intelligence transforms raw financial data into actionable insight. You will stop being a passive filer and become an active manager of your financial destiny.

Welcome to the new era of personal tax preparation—where accuracy is automatic, optimization is continuous, and stress is replaced by certainty. The algorithms are ready. The data is connected. The system is smarter than ever. Now it is time for you to use it.

Chapter 1

The Rise of AI in Personal Tax Preparation

The transformation of personal tax preparation did not begin with flashy apps or sleek dashboards—it began quietly, deep inside the financial systems that process trillions of dollars every year. Banks, payroll companies, investment platforms, and governments all struggled with the same problem: too much data moving too fast for humans to manage. Every paycheck, stock trade, crypto transaction, and expense receipt created a new line of tax-relevant information. For decades, this information had to be manually organized, verified, and reported, creating endless opportunities for errors, delays, and lost money. Artificial intelligence emerged as the only technology capable of handling this level of financial complexity at scale, and once it entered the tax world, everything changed.

At its core, AI tax preparation is about turning chaos into clarity. A modern taxpayer might have income from an employer, dividends from stocks, gains from crypto trades, rental income from property, and sales from an online store—all flowing through different platforms. Traditional tax software asks the user to type this information in manually, hoping nothing is forgotten or misclassified. AI systems do the opposite. They connect directly to data sources, pull transaction records automatically, and apply pattern recognition to identify what each payment represents. A deposit is not just a number; it is labeled as wages, rent, interest, royalties, or business income based on where it came from, how it behaves, and how similar transactions have been classified in millions of other tax returns.

Machine learning allows AI to become more accurate over time. Every time a return is filed, corrected, audited, or refunded, the system learns. It sees which classifications were accepted by the IRS, which deductions were allowed, and which patterns triggered scrutiny. This feedback loop trains the AI to make better decisions for the next taxpayer. Unlike traditional software that follows fixed rules written by programmers, AI adapts to reality. It notices that certain types of gig income are often misreported, that certain deductions are commonly overlooked, and that certain filing strategies consistently produce better outcomes. This learning process is what gives AI its edge.

One of the most powerful breakthroughs in AI tax preparation is automated reconciliation. Human filers must manually compare bank statements, pay stubs, brokerage reports, and receipts to ensure the numbers match. AI does this instantly. It cross-checks income reported by employers against deposits in your bank account. It matches investment gains against brokerage statements. It compares business expenses against merchant records. If something does not line up, the system flags it before the return is ever submitted. This reduces the risk of audits, penalties, and rejected filings while also ensuring that every legitimate dollar is counted.

Another critical advancement is intelligent deduction discovery. Most people have no idea which deductions they qualify for. They either forget them, misunderstand them, or never realize they exist. AI changes this by analyzing spending patterns and comparing them to millions of similar taxpayers. If you have home office expenses, vehicle usage, software subscriptions, or medical costs that qualify, the system detects them. It does not wait for you to ask—it finds them automatically. This is why AI-driven tax software consistently produces higher refunds or lower balances due than traditional methods.

Speed is the visible benefit, but accuracy is the real revolution. An AI system can process a full tax return in minutes not because it cuts corners, but because it runs thousands of calculations simultaneously. It checks compliance rules at the federal, state, and local levels. It applies tax brackets, phase-outs, and credit limitations in real time. It validates

Social Security numbers, income totals, and filing status combinations. By the time you see the final result, the system has already performed more analysis than a human preparer could do in days.

Perhaps most importantly, AI brings transparency to a process that has always felt opaque. Instead of trusting a black box or a human expert, you can see exactly how your tax outcome was calculated. Modern AI platforms explain which deductions were applied, which credits were used, and why certain strategies were chosen. This turns tax filing into an educational experience, helping you understand how your financial decisions affect your tax liability.

As AI continues to evolve, tax preparation becomes less about compliance and more about strategy. The system can simulate different scenarios—married filing jointly versus separately, taking standard versus itemized deductions, selling an asset now versus later—and show you the financial impact of each choice. This gives taxpayers unprecedented control over their financial futures. Taxes stop being something that happens to you and start becoming something you actively manage.

What we are witnessing is not just better software—it is a fundamental shift in how individuals interact with the tax system. AI removes the friction, fear, and guesswork that have defined tax season for generations. It replaces them with automation, insight, and optimization. The era of manual tax filing is ending, and a new era of intelligent financial management is taking its place.

"The Return That Changed Everything"

When Michael sat down at his kitchen table with a stack of unopened envelopes and a knot in his stomach, he already knew how the night would end. It was tax season, and like every year before it, it felt like a looming storm. W-2s from his job, 1099s from freelance work, statements from his small investment account, and a growing pile of receipts from his side business were scattered across the table. He had tried using tax software before, but it always felt like he was guessing, clicking through endless questions, never sure if he was doing it right. This year felt even worse because his finances had become more complicated than ever.

A friend had told him about a new AI-powered tax platform, but Michael was skeptical. He imagined another complicated system, just with a shinier interface. Still, he was tired of stress and decided to try it. He logged in, connected his bank account, payroll provider, and investment platform, and watched as the screen began to fill with data. Within seconds, the AI had pulled in every transaction from the past year, categorizing each one with eerie precision. His salary was labeled correctly. His freelance payments were grouped together. Even the small dividend from a stock he had almost forgotten about appeared on the screen.

Michael felt something strange as he watched the numbers organize themselves—relief. The chaos he had been staring at on the table was suddenly gone, replaced by clean, structured information. The AI flagged a missing form from one freelance client and even suggested where to download it. When he uploaded it, the system instantly updated his income totals. No spreadsheets, no guesswork, no manual entry.

Then something even more surprising happened. The AI began identifying deductions Michael had never claimed before. It noticed his home office expenses, his internet bill, the mileage from his client visits, and even the portion of his phone bill used for business. Each one appeared on the screen with a short explanation of why it qualified. Michael realized that for years, he had been overpaying simply because he did not know what he was allowed to deduct.

As the system finished its analysis, it ran multiple filing scenarios. It showed him how different choices would affect his tax bill, explaining each one in plain language. When the final number appeared, Michael stared at it in disbelief. Not only did he not owe money, but he was getting a refund—larger than any he had ever received. For the first time in his adult life, tax season did not feel like a punishment. It felt like clarity. He clicked "File," and the system confirmed that his return had been submitted, validated, and encrypted for security. No mailing forms. No waiting in fear. Just a simple confirmation that everything was done.

As Michael closed his laptop, he looked at the stack of papers still sitting on his table and laughed. They felt like artifacts from another era. In their place was something new: a quiet confidence that he finally understood his financial life. Taxes were no longer a mystery. With AI on his side, they had become something he could control.

Chapter 2

How AI Understands Your Income Better Than You Do

Income is the foundation of every tax return, yet it is also the area where most errors occur. People rarely earn money from just one source anymore. They receive salaries, bonuses, commissions, freelance payments, rental income, royalties, dividends, crypto gains, and side-hustle deposits that arrive from dozens of platforms. To a human, these numbers look like a messy stream of deposits. To an AI tax system, they form a pattern. Modern tax algorithms do not simply record income — they understand it. They analyze where money comes from, how often it appears, how it behaves over time, and how it compares to millions of similar taxpayers. This allows the system to classify income with a level of precision no human could ever achieve.

The reason this matters is that every type of income is taxed differently. W-2 wages follow one set of rules. 1099 freelance income follows another. Rental income, capital gains, dividends, crypto, and royalties all have their own treatments, thresholds, and deductions. Traditional tax software relies on the user to tell it what each payment represents. If you click the wrong box, your tax bill changes. AI removes this risk by learning the signature of each income type. It recognizes employer payroll patterns, gig-platform payouts, peer-to-peer transfers, brokerage settlements, crypto exchange activity, and marketplace sales. The system knows whether a payment is a gift, a refund, a business sale, or taxable income because it has seen millions of similar transactions before.

This intelligence allows AI to detect missing income automatically. If a bank deposit does not match any known source, the system flags it. If an employer reported income to the IRS that is not in your data feed, the system finds it. If a crypto exchange issued a tax form that you forgot to upload, the AI notices the gap. This protects you from underreporting, which is one of the most common triggers for IRS audits. Instead of hoping you remembered everything, you are backed by a system that compares your financial reality against government reporting databases.

AI also understands income timing. Humans tend to think in calendar years, but money does not always arrive neatly between January and December. Bonuses may be paid late, commissions may be delayed, and crypto transactions may settle on different days. AI systems track transaction timestamps, settlement dates, and reporting periods to ensure income is counted in the correct tax year. This prevents mistakes that could shift income into the wrong period and cause penalties or interest.

Another powerful feature is income normalization. AI compares your income profile to millions of similar taxpayers in your industry, region, and income bracket. If something looks unusual — such as unusually low income for a high-expense lifestyle or unusually high business revenue without corresponding costs — the system highlights it. This allows you to correct issues before filing and reduces the risk of scrutiny. It also helps detect fraud, identity theft, or reporting errors early.

For people with multiple income streams, this technology is transformative. A freelancer who earns from five platforms, a real estate investor with multiple properties, or a digital entrepreneur with global sales no longer has to manually reconcile dozens of statements. The AI aggregates everything into one coherent financial picture. It does not just show how much you earned — it shows how you earned it, when you earned it, and how it should be taxed.

This intelligence also allows AI to project future income. By analyzing historical trends, seasonality, and growth patterns, the system can estimate what your income will look like in the coming months. This is the foundation for tax forecasting, withholding optimization, and quarterly estimated payments.

Instead of being surprised by a large tax bill, you can adjust in real time.

Ultimately, income is no longer a static number on a form. In the age of AI, it is a living data stream that is constantly analyzed, verified, and optimized. When AI understands your income, it gives you control over your taxes before the bill ever arrives.

"The Invisible Income"

Sofia always thought she knew how much money she made. She worked full-time as a marketing manager, picked up freelance projects on the side, sold digital templates online, and had a small portfolio of dividend-paying stocks. In her mind, it all balanced out. She paid her taxes every year and rarely thought about it beyond that. But deep down, she felt uneasy because she never quite knew where all the money went.

When she tried an AI tax system for the first time, she expected a simple import of her W-2 and maybe her brokerage statement. What she did not expect was how deeply the system would see into her financial life. Within minutes, the dashboard displayed every stream of income she had, neatly categorized. Her salary sat in one column. Freelance payments in another. Digital product sales in a third. Even tiny dividend payments and interest earnings appeared, each one traced back to its source. Then the system flagged something. A few hundred dollars of income from a payment processor Sofia had forgotten about. It was from a client who had paid her late for a project she barely remembered. The AI had matched the deposit to a 1099 issued by the platform and pulled it into her return. Without the system, she never would have reported it, and she would have unknowingly risked an audit.

As Sofia scrolled through the income breakdown, she realized how fragmented her financial life had become. What felt like a few simple side hustles was actually a web of income streams, each with its own tax rules. The AI did not just list the numbers — it explained them. It showed her which income was self-employment, which was passive, and which qualified for special tax treatment.

By the time she reached the end of the analysis, Sofia felt something shift. She no longer felt confused about her money. She felt informed. The invisible income that had been scattered across accounts was now visible, organized, and understood. For the first time, she truly knew what she earned — and that knowledge gave her a sense of control she had never had before.

Chapter 3

How AI Eliminates Errors and Prevents IRS Problems

Tax mistakes are rarely intentional, but the IRS treats them all the same. A forgotten form, a misclassified expense, a mismatched income total, or a simple math error can trigger audits, penalties, interest, and months of stress. In the traditional tax system, accuracy depends almost entirely on human attention and memory. In the AI-driven system, accuracy is built into the architecture itself. Artificial intelligence does not rely on you to catch mistakes — it is constantly hunting for them in the background.

Every AI tax platform operates on multiple layers of validation. The first layer is mathematical integrity. Every number that enters the system is verified against its source. Bank deposits must match reported income. Brokerage statements must match capital gains. Payroll records must match W-2s. If anything does not align, the system flags it immediately. Humans often assume numbers are correct when they look reasonable, but AI checks them against independent sources, eliminating silent errors before they become legal problems. The second layer is rule-based compliance. AI systems contain complete digital versions of the tax code at the federal, state, and local levels. These are not just static rules — they are dynamic models that account for filing status, income thresholds, phaseouts, credits, and exceptions. When you enter or import data, the system instantly applies every relevant rule. It does not forget obscure regulations or misinterpret complex scenarios. It evaluates every possible requirement simultaneously, ensuring your return fits within the legal framework before it is ever submitted.

The third layer is anomaly detection. AI compares your tax profile against millions of similar taxpayers. If something looks unusual — unusually high deductions, missing income, mismatched totals, or strange filing patterns — the system notices. This does not mean you are wrong, but it gives you the chance to verify and document anything that could draw attention. Instead of being surprised by an IRS letter months later, you can address potential issues in advance.

AI also understands audit risk. By analyzing historical IRS enforcement data, the system knows which patterns are more likely to trigger scrutiny. It can warn you if a particular deduction or income classification increases your risk profile. It can even suggest alternative legal strategies that produce similar tax savings with lower audit probability. This is something no human preparer can do consistently because it requires analyzing massive datasets of enforcement outcomes.

Another powerful advantage is documentation. Every number on an AI-generated return is linked to a data source. If the IRS ever asks for proof, the system can retrieve bank records, receipts, transaction logs, and reports automatically. This creates a digital audit trail that protects you. You no longer have to dig through old emails or shoeboxes of paper. Your entire tax history becomes searchable and defensible.

As tax systems become more automated on the government side, this accuracy becomes even more important. The IRS increasingly uses AI to cross-check filings against third-party data. When both sides use intelligent systems, mismatches are detected faster than ever. Filing with AI ensures that your data aligns with what banks, employers, and platforms have reported, dramatically reducing the risk of automated enforcement actions.

What AI ultimately provides is peace of mind. You are no longer relying on luck or memory. You are supported by a system that was designed to find errors before they cost you money or sleep. In the modern tax world, intelligence is protection, and AI is the most powerful shield you can have.

"The Letter That Never Came"

David used to dread the mail. Every time an envelope from the IRS arrived, his stomach tightened. Years ago, a small mistake on a return had spiraled into months of back-and-forth letters, penalties, and stress. Ever since then, tax season felt like walking through a minefield. Even when he filed on time, he always wondered if something was wrong.

This year, he decided to try an AI tax system. He uploaded his documents, connected his accounts, and waited. What surprised him was not the speed, but the warnings. The system flagged a deduction he had claimed in the past that was no longer allowed under current rules. It also noticed a mismatch between a 1099 and a bank deposit. David corrected both with a few clicks, grateful that the issues were caught before they could become problems.

When he filed, the system generated a complete audit trail — every number, every source, every calculation documented and stored. For the first time, he felt confident instead of anxious.

Months passed. April turned into May. Then June. No letters. No notices. No threats. Just silence.

One day, David realized something profound. He was no longer afraid of his own tax return. The invisible shield of AI had done what years of worry never could — it gave him peace.

Chapter 4

How AI Tracks Expenses, Builds Perfect Records, and Turns Data Into Deductions

For decades, expense tracking has been the weakest link in personal tax preparation. Income is usually reported by someone else — employers, banks, platforms, or brokers — but expenses depend almost entirely on the taxpayer. Receipts are lost, transactions are forgotten, and deductions disappear simply because there is no reliable system to capture them. This is where artificial intelligence creates one of its most dramatic advantages. AI does not wait for you to remember your expenses. It observes, records, categorizes, and preserves them automatically, building a living financial record that is always tax-ready.

Traditional expense tracking relies on human behavior. You are expected to save receipts, log mileage, separate personal and business purchases, and remember what each transaction was for months later. AI removes this burden by integrating directly with your financial ecosystem. It connects to bank accounts, credit cards, payment processors, invoicing systems, and digital wallets. Every transaction is captured at the moment it occurs. The system analyzes merchant data, transaction descriptions, purchase frequency, and historical behavior to determine whether an expense is personal, business-related, deductible, partially deductible, or non-deductible. This happens continuously, not once a year.

Machine learning gives AI the ability to recognize expense patterns that humans overlook. If you consistently purchase software subscriptions, professional services, office supplies, or educational tools, the system learns that these are recurring business expenses. If you pay for fuel, vehicle maintenance, or travel tied to income-producing activity, the system tracks mileage, dates, and locations. Over time, AI builds a behavioral map of your financial life, allowing it to categorize expenses with increasing accuracy. What begins as automation quickly becomes intelligence.

One of the most powerful features of AI-driven expense tracking is contextual understanding. AI does not just see a transaction — it understands its purpose. A meal purchased near a client meeting, a flight booked during a business trip, or a hotel stay aligned with conference dates are all evaluated in context. The system cross-references calendars, emails, invoices, and location data when available to determine whether an expense qualifies. This level of analysis allows deductions that would otherwise be missed or incorrectly excluded.

AI also solves one of the most dangerous problems in tax filing: inconsistent records. Many audits are triggered not by large deductions, but by sloppy documentation. When expenses do not align with income, business activity, or prior filings, the return attracts attention. AI prevents this by maintaining consistency across time. It ensures that expenses scale logically with income, that categories remain stable year over year, and that documentation exists for every claimed deduction. The result is a clean, defensible return that looks credible to both human reviewers and automated IRS systems.

Another critical advantage is real-time visibility. Instead of discovering your deductions after the year ends, AI shows them to you as they accumulate. You can see how much you have spent in each category, how it affects your tax position, and whether you are missing opportunities. This transforms tax preparation into tax management. You can adjust behavior mid-year — delaying or accelerating expenses, upgrading tools, or restructuring spending — with immediate awareness of the tax impact.

AI also preserves records in a way humans never could. Receipts are digitized, tagged, and stored securely. Transaction histories are preserved even if accounts are closed or cards are replaced. If the IRS ever requests proof, the system can retrieve years of documentation instantly. This permanence is critical because audits often occur long after the return is filed. With AI, your records do not decay — they compound in value.

For self-employed individuals, freelancers, investors, and gig workers, this capability is transformative. Expenses that once required discipline and manual effort become effortless. The system works silently in the background, ensuring that nothing is lost and nothing is exaggerated. Accuracy replaces approximation. Confidence replaces uncertainty.

Ultimately, AI turns expense tracking from a chore into a strategic advantage. It ensures that every legitimate deduction is captured, supported, and optimized. It builds a financial record that is not only compliant, but intelligent. In the modern tax environment, data is power, and AI is the system that turns raw transactions into financial leverage.

"Seven Receipts and a Lifetime of Stress"

Elena had always believed she was bad with money. Not reckless — just disorganized. Her income was steady, her bills were paid, but when tax season arrived, everything fell apart. Receipts were scattered across drawers, old purses, email inboxes, and glove compartments. Some were faded. Some were lost entirely. Every year, she promised herself it would be different. Every year, it wasn't. Elena ran a small consulting business from home while juggling family responsibilities and a demanding schedule. She knew she had expenses that should be deductible — software, supplies, internet, phone usage, travel — but proving it felt impossible. By the time she sat down to file her taxes, the details were blurry. What was business? What was personal? What could she justify? What would trigger trouble? The fear of making a mistake led her to underclaim deductions, quietly paying more tax than she should have just to feel safe.

One night, after another exhausting attempt to organize her paperwork, Elena discovered an AI-powered tax system recommended by another consultant. Skeptical but desperate, she signed up. The setup took less than an hour. She connected her bank accounts, credit cards, and payment platforms. Then she closed her laptop and forgot about it.

What Elena did not realize was that her financial life had just been quietly reorganized.

Weeks later, she opened the app out of curiosity. The screen displayed a complete breakdown of her expenses — categorized, labeled, and explained. Software subscriptions were already marked as business tools. Office supplies were grouped and tracked. Internet and phone bills were partially allocated based on usage patterns. Travel expenses were linked to client invoices and meeting dates. Even meals she had forgotten about were flagged with notes explaining why they qualified or didn't.

Elena felt a strange mix of disbelief and relief. For years, she had blamed herself for not being disciplined enough. Now she realized the system had simply been stacked against her. Humans were never meant to remember thousands of micro-transactions over twelve months. AI was.

As the year progressed, the system continued to work in silence. Every purchase was captured. Every receipt was stored. Every category grew more accurate. Elena began checking her dashboard monthly, watching her deductible expenses accumulate. For the first time, she could see her tax position forming in real time. She made smarter decisions — upgrading software when it made sense, timing purchases strategically, and understanding how each choice affected her bottom line.

When tax season arrived, there was no panic. No stacks of paper. No frantic searches. The system generated her return with every expense already accounted for, supported by a digital trail that stretched back through the entire year. Her refund was larger than it had ever been.

But the real change was not financial — it was emotional.

Months later, when a friend mentioned an IRS audit horror story, Elena realized something shocking. She was not afraid. Every transaction in her return was documented. Every deduction was justified. Every record was preserved. If a letter ever came, she knew exactly how she would respond.

Elena still remembered the seven receipts she once held in her hand, trying to reconstruct a year of work from fading ink. She smiled, knowing that chapter of her life was over. The stress that had followed her for decades had disappeared — not because she became better with money, but because she finally had a system that was.

Chapter 5

How AI Transforms Taxes for Gig Workers, Freelancers, and 1099 Earners

The rise of the gig economy has permanently reshaped how people earn money, but the tax system has struggled to keep up. Millions of individuals now earn income through freelancing platforms, contract work, digital marketplaces, ride-sharing apps, content creation, consulting, online sales, and remote services. While this flexibility has unlocked new opportunities, it has also created unprecedented tax complexity. Gig workers are suddenly responsible for tracking income, expenses, deductions, estimated payments, and compliance rules that traditional employees never have to think about. Artificial intelligence is the first technology capable of truly solving this problem at scale.

At the heart of the challenge is fragmentation. A single gig worker might earn money from multiple platforms, receive payments through different processors, incur expenses across dozens of categories, and operate across state or even national lines. Each platform reports income differently. Some issue 1099s. Some do not. Some report gross income. Others report net payouts. Humans are expected to reconcile all of this manually, often months after the fact. AI eliminates this fragmentation by acting as a central intelligence layer that unifies every income stream into one coherent system.

AI tax platforms connect directly to gig marketplaces, payment processors, bank accounts, invoicing tools, and digital wallets. They continuously ingest transaction data, identifying which deposits represent taxable income and which are reimbursements, transfers, or refunds. Unlike traditional software that waits for tax forms, AI builds your income record in real time. This means that by the time tax season arrives, your income is already categorized, verified, and reconciled.

One of the most important advantages AI provides to gig workers is self-employment tax optimization. Many freelancers are shocked when they discover they owe not only income tax, but also self-employment tax. AI systems calculate this automatically and track it throughout the year. They estimate quarterly payments, forecast year-end liability, and show how deductions and expenses reduce both income tax and self-employment tax simultaneously. This visibility allows gig workers to plan instead of panic.

AI also excels at expense matching for gig work. Every platform has its own expense profile. Ride-share drivers incur fuel, maintenance, insurance, and mileage. Freelancers incur software, equipment, education, and home office costs. Content creators incur tools, subscriptions, travel, and marketing expenses. AI learns these patterns and applies them intelligently. It knows which expenses are common, which are rare, and which require documentation. This ensures deductions are maximized while remaining defensible.

Another transformative feature is income smoothing and volatility management. Gig income is rarely consistent. One month may be lucrative, the next slow. AI analyzes income trends, identifies seasonality, and helps forecast tax obligations based on realistic averages rather than emotional guesswork. This is especially important for estimated quarterly payments, which are a major source of penalties for freelancers. By projecting income forward, AI helps avoid underpayment and overpayment alike.

AI also handles multi-state and platform-specific rules with ease. A freelancer may live in one state, work for clients in several others, and earn income through platforms headquartered elsewhere. Human filers often misunderstand which income is taxed where. AI applies sourcing rules, nexus thresholds, and reporting requirements automatically. It knows when state filings are required and when they are not, reducing compliance risk without unnecessary filings.

Perhaps most importantly, AI gives gig workers confidence. The psychological burden of self-employment taxes is immense. Many freelancers undercharge, overwork, or avoid growth because they fear tax consequences. AI removes that fear by making the system transparent. You can see exactly how much you owe, why you owe it, and how to reduce it legally. This turns tax knowledge into business leverage.

In the AI era, gig workers no longer have to operate in financial uncertainty. They can grow income streams, add platforms, and scale operations with clarity instead of fear. AI transforms self-employment taxes from a liability into a manageable, optimized system that supports independence rather than punishes it.

"The Year Marcus Finally Breathed"

Marcus never planned to become a freelancer. It happened slowly. First, a side project for a friend. Then a contract that paid more than his salary. Then another. Within a year, his full-time job was gone, replaced by a patchwork of clients, platforms, and projects that paid well but felt unstable. Everyone congratulated him on his freedom, but no one saw the anxiety that followed him every night.

The money came in waves. Some months were incredible. Others were terrifying. Marcus kept telling himself he would "figure out taxes later," but later always arrived with dread. He had no employer withholding money. No clear sense of what he owed. No idea which expenses counted or how much to save. He opened a separate savings account labeled "Taxes" and dumped money into it randomly, hoping it would be enough.

When tax season finally arrived, Marcus panicked. Forms arrived from some platforms but not others. Bank statements showed deposits he could not easily categorize. Expenses were scattered across cards and accounts. He spent hours reading conflicting advice online, each article making things worse. He felt like he had built a career without understanding the rules that governed it.

A fellow freelancer recommended an AI tax system, calling it "the thing that saved my sanity." Marcus was skeptical but exhausted. He signed up.

The system asked him to connect his accounts. He did, half-expecting nothing to happen. Then the dashboard began to populate. Every platform he used appeared automatically. Each deposit was labeled with its source and type. Income streams he had mentally lumped together were separated and explained. The chaos of the past year began to resolve into something coherent.

Then came the expenses.

The AI had already identified software subscriptions, cloud services, equipment purchases, internet costs, phone usage, travel expenses, and education tools Marcus had forgotten he bought. Each one appeared with a note explaining why it qualified and how it reduced both income tax and self-employment tax. Marcus stared at the screen, realizing how much money he had left on the table in previous years simply because he did not know.

But the real shift came when the system projected his future.

The AI analyzed his income patterns, showing seasonal dips and spikes. It estimated his quarterly payments for the upcoming year and explained how they were calculated. It even suggested setting aside a specific percentage of each payment instead of guessing. Suddenly, taxes were no longer a looming unknown. They were a predictable system.

As months passed, Marcus checked the dashboard regularly. It became a quiet companion rather than a source of fear. He saw his tax liability rise and fall in real time. He made smarter decisions — timing equipment purchases, setting rates confidently, accepting new clients without fear of surprise bills.

When tax season returned, it felt anticlimactic. The return was already built. Every number was documented. Every deduction was supported. Marcus clicked file and closed his laptop without the usual knot in his stomach.

Later that night, sitting on his balcony, Marcus realized something profound. For the first time since going freelance, he felt calm. Not rich. Not invincible. Just steady. The freedom he had chased was finally real — not because he earned more, but because he understood the system that governed his success.

He took a deep breath, smiled, and let the fear go.

Chapter 6

How AI Handles Real Estate, Crypto, and Investment Taxes Without Guesswork

For most taxpayers, real estate, cryptocurrency, and investment income represent the point where taxes shift from mildly confusing to overwhelmingly complex. These assets operate under entirely different tax rules than wages or freelance income, involving depreciation schedules, capital gains classifications, holding periods, cost basis tracking, passive activity rules, wash sales, and constantly changing regulations. Even experienced accountants can struggle to manage these elements accurately, especially when transactions span multiple platforms, years, and asset types. Artificial intelligence changes this landscape by doing what humans cannot: continuously tracking, reconciling, and optimizing complex asset data across time.

Real estate taxation alone is a maze. Rental income must be reported, but so must expenses, depreciation, repairs, improvements, and financing costs. Each category is treated differently by the tax code. A repair may be deductible immediately, while an improvement must be depreciated over decades. Depreciation itself introduces another layer of complexity, as it reduces taxable income without affecting cash flow, while also impacting capital gains when a property is sold. AI systems are uniquely suited to manage this complexity because they track every property as a living financial entity, not just a line item on a return.

AI-driven tax platforms connect to property management software, banking records, mortgage statements, and expense accounts to build a complete picture of each property's financial activity. They automatically distinguish between repairs and capital improvements based on transaction data, vendor behavior, and historical patterns. Depreciation schedules are calculated precisely, adjusted when improvements are added, and carried forward year after year without error. When a property is sold, the system already knows the adjusted basis, accumulated depreciation, and holding period, allowing it to calculate capital gains accurately and apply the correct tax treatment.

Cryptocurrency introduces an entirely different challenge. Every trade, swap, sale, transfer, or conversion can be a taxable event. Cost basis must be tracked across wallets and exchanges, often involving thousands of micro-transactions. Humans are simply not equipped to reconstruct this data manually, especially when platforms use different reporting standards or fail to provide complete records. AI excels here by connecting directly to exchanges, wallets, and blockchains, ingesting raw transaction data, and reconstructing cost basis with mathematical precision.

AI systems classify crypto transactions intelligently. They distinguish between trades, transfers, staking rewards, mining income, airdrops, and forks. They apply the correct tax treatment to each event based on jurisdiction and current law. Holding periods are tracked down to the second, ensuring gains are classified as short-term or long-term correctly. When transactions span multiple wallets, the AI follows the digital trail automatically, eliminating gaps that often trigger audits.

Investment taxes add yet another layer of complexity. Stocks, bonds, ETFs, mutual funds, options, and alternative investments all generate different types of taxable events. Dividends may be qualified or ordinary. Capital gains may be realized or unrealized. Wash sale rules can disallow losses without proper tracking. AI systems monitor investment activity continuously, tracking cost basis, reinvestments, splits, and corporate actions. They detect wash sales automatically and adjust loss calculations accordingly, something even sophisticated investors often miss. One of the most powerful capabilities of AI in this area is scenario modeling. The system can simulate the tax impact of selling an asset now versus later, harvesting losses, or restructuring a portfolio. It can show how selling a property this year versus next year affects taxes, how depreciation recapture will apply, and how gains interact with other income. This transforms tax filing into tax strategy. Instead of reacting to transactions after they occur, you can plan them intelligently.

AI also brings clarity to passive activity rules and income thresholds that confuse many investors. It understands when rental losses can offset other income and when they must be carried forward. It applies income limits, material participation tests, and special allowances automatically. This ensures compliance while maximizing legal tax benefits.

The common thread across real estate, crypto, and investments is continuity. These assets generate tax consequences over years or decades, not just one filing season. AI preserves institutional memory. It remembers what you paid, what you deducted, what you depreciated, and how rules applied in prior years. This continuity is what makes accurate long-term tax optimization possible.

Without AI, taxpayers rely on fragmented records, outdated spreadsheets, and fallible memory. With AI, complex assets become manageable, transparent, and strategically optimized. The system does not just report what happened — it understands it, preserves it, and uses it to protect and grow your wealth over time.

"The Ledger That Never Forgot"

When Daniel bought his first rental property, he thought the hard part was over. The mortgage was approved. The tenant was in place. The rent checks arrived on time. To Daniel, the property felt like success — tangible, reliable, and finally working for him. What he did not anticipate was the silent complexity that followed him into tax season.

At first, it seemed manageable. He reported the rental income. He deducted some expenses. His accountant asked questions Daniel struggled to answer. Was that expense a repair or an improvement? Did that trip count as business travel? How much depreciation had he taken last year? Daniel shrugged, trusting the professional to figure it out. Over time, the questions multiplied, and the answers became guesswork.

Then Daniel discovered crypto.

What began as curiosity turned into active trading. He bought, sold, swapped, transferred, and staked across multiple exchanges. At the time, it felt harmless — just numbers moving on a screen. But when tax season arrived, it felt like a reckoning. Spreadsheets exploded. Exchange reports contradicted each other. Wallet transfers looked like taxable events. Daniel spent nights trying to reconstruct a financial history he had never meant to track.

The breaking point came when his accountant admitted uncertainty. "We'll do our best," she said, "but crypto is messy."

That was when Daniel decided something had to change.

A fellow investor introduced him to an AI-powered tax system, describing it as "a ledger that never forgets." Skeptical but desperate, Daniel signed up. The system asked him to connect his accounts — property management software, banks, mortgage lenders, crypto exchanges, wallets, and brokerage platforms. Daniel expected chaos. Instead, he watched clarity unfold.

The AI built a profile for each rental property, tracking income, expenses, depreciation, and loan interest automatically. Repairs were categorized correctly. Improvements were capitalized. Depreciation schedules updated themselves silently in the background. For the first time, Daniel could see the true performance of each property, not just in cash flow, but in tax impact.

Then came the crypto. Thousands of transactions appeared, each one traced back to its origin. Transfers between wallets were identified correctly. Trades were classified. Holding periods were calculated. Gains and losses emerged from the noise like constellations forming in the dark. What had once felt impossible was now simply... done.

As the year progressed, Daniel began using the system proactively. Before selling an asset, he checked the tax impact. Before making a major improvement, he saw how depreciation would change. Before trading crypto, he understood how timing affected his liability. Taxes were no longer something that happened after the fact — they were part of the decision-making process.

Months later, when he filed his return, there was no uncertainty. Every number had a history. Every deduction had support. Every gain was accounted for. The system generated a complete audit trail that stretched back years, not because Daniel had been disciplined, but because the AI had been relentless.

Sitting at his desk after filing, Daniel felt something unfamiliar: trust. Not blind trust in a professional or a spreadsheet, but trust in a system that remembered what humans could not. His investments no longer felt fragile. They felt grounded.

He realized then that wealth was not just about owning assets. It was about understanding them — and protecting them over time. And for the first time, Daniel knew he had a partner that would never forget.

Chapter 7

How AI Forecasts Taxes, Optimizes Withholding, and Eliminates Surprise Bills

For most people, the most painful part of taxes is not filing the return — it is the surprise. The unexpected bill. The sudden realization that too little was withheld, that estimated payments were wrong, or that income grew faster than planning kept up with. Traditional tax preparation is backward-looking by design. It tells you what already happened, long after decisions were made and money was spent. Artificial intelligence fundamentally changes this by turning taxes into a forward-looking system. Instead of reacting to outcomes, AI allows taxpayers to forecast, adjust, and optimize continuously.

Tax forecasting begins with pattern recognition. AI systems analyze years of historical income, expenses, deductions, credits, and filing outcomes to build a personalized financial model. This model is not static. It updates every time new income arrives, an expense is logged, or a transaction occurs. The system understands seasonality, volatility, growth trends, and behavioral patterns unique to each taxpayer. This allows it to predict not just how much tax you will owe, but when and why that liability is forming.

Withholding optimization is one of the most powerful applications of this forecasting ability. For employees, withholding is often set once and forgotten. Life changes — raises, bonuses, side income, investments — but withholding does not adjust automatically. AI monitors these changes in real time. If additional income pushes you into a higher bracket, the system detects the shortfall early. If deductions increase or credits apply, it identifies opportunities to reduce withholding. Instead of guessing or relying on generic calculators, AI recommends precise adjustments based on your actual financial behavior.

For self-employed individuals and investors, forecasting is even more critical. Estimated quarterly payments are one of the most common sources of penalties and cash flow stress. AI systems project income across the year, smoothing volatility and accounting for realistic fluctuations. They calculate estimated payments dynamically, adjusting recommendations as income rises or falls. This prevents both underpayment penalties and overpayment, ensuring money stays working for you instead of sitting idle with the government.

Another key advantage of AI forecasting is scenario

simulation. The system can model different outcomes before decisions are made. What happens if you sell an asset this year instead of next? What if you increase contributions to retirement accounts? What if income spikes unexpectedly? AI runs these scenarios instantly, showing the tax impact of each choice. This empowers proactive decision-making rather than reactive problem-solving.

AI also integrates tax forecasting with broader financial planning. Taxes do not exist in isolation. They interact with retirement contributions, investment strategies, healthcare costs, education planning, and cash flow management. AI systems coordinate these elements, ensuring that tax optimization aligns with long-term goals rather than short-term fixes. This holistic view prevents strategies that reduce taxes today but create problems tomorrow.

Perhaps the most transformative effect of AI forecasting is psychological. Tax anxiety often stems from uncertainty. Not knowing what is coming creates fear and avoidance. AI replaces uncertainty with visibility. You can see your projected tax position at any point in the year. You know whether you are ahead, behind, or exactly on track. This clarity reduces stress and encourages better financial habits.

As governments continue to automate enforcement and reporting, proactive compliance becomes essential. AI forecasting ensures alignment between what you owe and what is paid throughout the year. It minimizes surprises, penalties, and interest while maximizing control. Taxes stop being a once-a-year reckoning and become an integrated part of financial life.

In the AI era, tax forecasting is not a luxury — it is a necessity. Those who rely on backward-looking systems will continue to be surprised. Those who adopt AI will operate with foresight, precision, and confidence.

"The April That Never Hurt"

April used to feel like a cliff.

For years, Natalie approached tax season with the same uneasy ritual. She would file on time, hoping for the best, bracing for the worst. Some years she owed a little. Other years she owed a lot. No matter the outcome, it always felt disconnected from her actual life. She earned more, worked harder, and tried to be responsible — yet taxes still felt like punishment rather than calculation.

Natalie was a high-performing professional with a growing career, bonuses that fluctuated wildly, investment income that crept upward each year, and a side project that had quietly become profitable. On paper, she was doing everything right. Emotionally, she felt constantly unprepared. She never knew if she was saving enough. She never knew if withholding was correct. She never knew if success would come with a bill attached.

The worst year came without warning.

A large bonus arrived late in the year. Natalie celebrated, paid off debt, invested, and traveled. Then April arrived. The tax bill erased the joy of that bonus in a single moment. She felt blindsided, even though nothing illegal or unusual had happened. The system simply moved faster than her awareness.

That was the year Natalie decided she would never be surprised again.

A colleague mentioned an AI tax system that "shows you the future instead of scolding you about the past." The phrase stuck with her. Natalie signed up, not expecting much beyond better organization. What she got was something else entirely.

The first thing the system showed her was a projection. Not last year's numbers — this year's trajectory. It analyzed her salary, bonus structure, investment income, and side earnings.

It showed her where she stood today and where she would likely land by December. A line chart traced her tax liability as it formed, slowly and predictably.

Natalie stared at the screen, realizing she had never seen her taxes this way before. Not as a mystery, but as a process unfolding in real time.

When a bonus hit mid-year, the system updated instantly. A notification explained how the additional income affected her bracket and how much extra withholding would keep her on track. It offered a recommendation — not a demand — with clear reasoning behind it. Natalie adjusted her withholding with confidence instead of fear.

Later that year, she considered selling some investments. Before making the move, she ran a simulation. The AI showed her the tax impact now versus later, how gains would interact with her income, and how timing could reduce the burden. For the first time, she made a financial decision knowing the tax consequences before they happened.

Months passed, and something subtle changed. Natalie stopped dreading money conversations. She checked her dashboard the way someone checks the weather — not obsessively, but calmly. She knew what was coming. She knew what to expect. Taxes were no longer a looming threat. They were simply part of the map.

April arrived quietly. Natalie filed her return without holding her breath. The numbers matched the forecast almost exactly. No shock. No sting. No regret. She closed her laptop and realized something remarkable — tax season had passed without emotional damage.

That night, Natalie thought back to all the Aprils that had hurt. All the anxiety, the surprises, the self-blame. None of it had been necessary. She had never lacked discipline or intelligence. She had lacked visibility.

Now she had it.

And with that clarity came something even more valuable than savings or refunds — peace.

Chapter 8

How AI Stays Current With Tax Law, Ensures Compliance, and Protects You From Costly Mistakes

Tax law is not a fixed rulebook. It is a living, constantly changing system shaped by legislation, court rulings, regulatory guidance, administrative interpretation, and enforcement priorities. Every year, thousands of changes ripple through the tax code—some large and headline-grabbing, others small but financially significant. Phaseouts shift. Credits appear or disappear. Thresholds adjust for inflation. Reporting requirements evolve. For human taxpayers and even professionals, keeping up is nearly impossible. Artificial intelligence changes this dynamic by treating tax law not as a static reference, but as a continuously updated operating system.

At the core of AI-driven tax compliance is real-time legal ingestion. Modern AI systems are designed to monitor legislative updates, IRS notices, revenue procedures, tax court decisions, and regulatory bulletins as they are released. These updates are parsed, categorized, and mapped to specific taxpayer scenarios. Instead of waiting for annual software updates or relying on outdated guidance, AI incorporates legal changes immediately. This ensures that your tax calculations reflect the most current rules available at the moment you file.

One of the most critical compliance advantages AI provides is interpretation at scale. Tax law is filled with gray areas, exceptions, and conditional logic. Human interpretation is subjective and inconsistent. AI models are trained on vast libraries of historical filings, enforcement actions, and judicial outcomes. This allows them to infer how rules are applied in practice, not just how they are written. When a deduction or credit has nuanced requirements, the AI evaluates eligibility probabilistically based on real-world outcomes, not just theoretical definitions.

AI also enforces consistency across filings. Many compliance issues arise not from blatant errors, but from subtle inconsistencies year over year. A deduction claimed one year but not the next. A business classification that quietly changes. An income stream reported differently over time. AI systems track your historical filings and ensure that changes are intentional, documented, and justified. This continuity dramatically reduces audit risk, because the IRS increasingly relies on automated systems to detect anomalies. Another powerful feature of AI compliance is jurisdictional awareness. Tax rules vary across federal, state, and local levels, and they often interact in complex ways. A deduction allowed federally may be limited or disallowed at the state level. Credits may exist in one jurisdiction but not another. AI systems apply layered compliance automatically, ensuring that each return meets the specific requirements of every relevant authority. This is especially valuable for taxpayers with multi-state activity, remote work arrangements, or investment income across regions.

AI also excels at compliance documentation. When a rule requires substantiation, the system ensures that supporting records exist and are linked to the return. It flags missing documentation before filing, reducing the chance of future disputes. If guidance changes after a return is filed, AI can assess whether an amended return is beneficial or necessary. This proactive approach prevents small compliance issues from becoming expensive problems.

As governments themselves adopt AI for enforcement, alignment becomes critical. The IRS increasingly uses machine learning to cross-check third-party data, detect inconsistencies, and prioritize audits. Filing with AI ensures that your return speaks the same "language" as enforcement systems. Data formats align. Calculations match reported sources. Discrepancies are minimized. This reduces the likelihood of automated flags and correspondence audits.

Beyond technical compliance, AI provides education. Instead of simply applying rules silently, modern systems explain why certain items are included or excluded. This transparency helps taxpayers understand their obligations and avoid repeated mistakes. Over time, users become more informed and proactive, strengthening compliance behavior naturally.

Ultimately, AI transforms tax law from an unpredictable threat into a managed system. You are no longer exposed to the risk of missing changes, misinterpreting rules, or relying on outdated knowledge. Compliance becomes continuous rather than annual. Protection becomes structural rather than reactive. In a world where tax law grows more complex every year, AI is the only tool capable of keeping pace.

"The Rule That Changed Overnight"

The email arrived on a Tuesday morning, quietly slipping into Karen's inbox between client messages and meeting reminders. It was from the IRS.

Her heart sank.

Karen was not reckless. She had always filed her taxes carefully, using reputable software and occasionally consulting professionals. She ran a small but growing online education business, reported her income honestly, and kept what she thought were decent records. Still, the subject line—*Notice of Adjustment*—felt like a verdict before she had even opened it.

The issue was not fraud or deception. It was something far more frustrating: a rule change.

A deduction Karen had claimed—one she had taken for years—had been quietly modified by updated guidance. The change was subtle, buried in regulatory language she never would have seen. Her return was technically incorrect under the new interpretation, even though it had been acceptable before. The result was a reassessment, interest, and a request for documentation she was not sure she still had.

Karen felt betrayed by a system that changed the rules without warning.

The months that followed were exhausting. Letters. Phone calls. Uncertainty. She paid what was owed just to make it stop, but the experience left a scar. She realized that compliance was no longer about honesty or effort—it was about awareness. And awareness was something she did not have.

The following year, a fellow business owner suggested an AI-based tax platform. Karen was skeptical. Software had failed her before. Still, the promise of "continuous compliance" intrigued her. She signed up, half expecting disappointment.

The first thing the system did was review her prior returns.

It flagged the very deduction that had caused her trouble, explaining in plain language how the rule had changed and why it now required additional criteria. The AI showed her exactly where her filing would have conflicted with current guidance. Karen stared at the screen, stunned. The system had identified the issue before she even thought to look for it.

As the year progressed, Karen noticed something new. The platform sent occasional notifications—not alarms, but updates. A reporting threshold changed. A credit phaseout adjusted. A documentation requirement tightened. Each message explained what changed, who it affected, and whether Karen needed to act. Most of the time, the answer was no. But the knowledge itself was empowering.

Midway through the year, Karen considered expanding her business into another state. Before she did, she ran a compliance check. The AI showed her potential filing obligations, registration thresholds, and tax implications. What could have become a costly oversight became a planned decision.

When tax season arrived, Karen felt something she had not felt in years: confidence. The return was generated with every rule applied correctly, every update accounted for, every requirement met. The system explained why certain deductions were allowed and why others were limited. It linked documentation automatically. It even noted where recent guidance had influenced calculations.

Karen filed without hesitation.

Months passed. No letters. No notices. No surprises.

One evening, as she closed her laptop after checking her dashboard, Karen realized how much had changed. The fear that once accompanied tax season was gone. She was no longer trying to memorize rules or hope nothing had changed. She had a system that watched the rules for her.

The tax code would continue to evolve. That much was inevitable.

But for the first time, Karen knew she would evolve with it—quietly, continuously, and safely.

Chapter 9

How AI Integrates Taxes With Financial Planning and Protects Long-Term Wealth

For most people, taxes and financial planning exist in separate mental compartments. Taxes are something handled once a year, often under pressure, while financial planning is treated as a long-term, abstract goal focused on retirement, savings, and investments. This separation is one of the most expensive mistakes individuals make over a lifetime. Taxes are not a side effect of financial decisions—they are one of the primary forces shaping wealth accumulation. Artificial intelligence bridges this divide by integrating tax intelligence directly into financial planning, transforming isolated decisions into a coordinated strategy that protects and compounds wealth over time.

At its foundation, AI-driven financial integration begins with a unified financial model. Instead of viewing income, expenses, investments, retirement accounts, and taxes as separate systems, AI treats them as interconnected variables. Every decision—earning more, investing differently, contributing to retirement, selling assets, or reallocating capital—has tax consequences that ripple across time. AI systems model these interactions continuously, showing how today's decisions affect tomorrow's outcomes. This eliminates blind spots that traditional planning tools cannot see.

One of the most powerful areas of integration is retirement planning. Contributions to retirement accounts affect taxable income today, investment growth over time, and withdrawal taxation in the future. AI analyzes these trade-offs dynamically. It can recommend optimal contribution levels across different account types—traditional, Roth, taxable—based on current income, expected future income, tax brackets, and legislative risk. Rather than following generic advice, taxpayers receive personalized strategies that evolve as circumstances change.

Investment strategy is another area where AI integration delivers profound benefits. Capital gains timing, asset location, dividend treatment, and loss harvesting all interact with tax liability. AI systems monitor portfolios in real time, identifying opportunities to harvest losses, rebalance assets, or defer gains strategically. These actions are evaluated not just for immediate tax savings, but for long-term impact on net worth. By coordinating investment decisions with tax forecasting, AI ensures that growth is preserved rather than eroded by unnecessary taxation. AI also plays a critical role in wealth protection. Taxes are often the largest predictable expense over a lifetime, and poor planning can quietly drain wealth even when investments perform well. AI models lifetime tax exposure under different scenarios, helping individuals choose paths that minimize cumulative tax burden. This includes planning for major life events—career changes, business exits, real estate sales, inheritance, and retirement transitions. By simulating these events in advance, AI allows for strategic positioning rather than reactive damage control.

Another advantage of AI integration is risk management. Financial plans often assume stable rules, but tax laws change. AI systems incorporate legislative risk into their models, stress-testing strategies against potential policy shifts. This helps avoid over-reliance on fragile tax advantages and encourages diversification of tax exposure. The goal is not just optimization, but resilience.

AI also enhances intergenerational planning. Wealth transfer involves estate taxes, gift taxes, basis adjustments, and long-term planning horizons that span decades. AI can model how assets grow, how taxes apply at each stage, and how different transfer strategies affect heirs. This allows families to preserve wealth across generations with clarity and intention.

Perhaps most importantly, AI integration changes behavior. When individuals can see the long-term tax impact of everyday decisions, they make better choices naturally. Spending, saving, investing, and earning become aligned with broader goals rather than short-term impulses. Financial planning stops being theoretical and becomes actionable.

In this integrated system, taxes are no longer a penalty for success—they are a design constraint that can be managed intelligently. AI transforms financial planning from fragmented guesswork into a cohesive, adaptive strategy that protects wealth not just this year, but for decades to come.

"The Long View"

For most of her adult life, Priya believed she was doing everything right.

She earned a strong income, saved diligently, invested consistently, and avoided unnecessary debt. Friends often described her as "financially disciplined," and on the surface, it was true. Yet beneath that discipline was a quiet frustration she could never quite articulate. No matter how much she earned or invested, she always felt like something was leaking—like progress required more effort than it should.

Taxes were part of that unease.

Every year, Priya filed accurately and on time. Some years she owed. Some years she didn't. But the outcome always felt disconnected from her broader goals. She was saving for retirement, helping family members, investing for the future—yet taxes seemed to operate in a separate universe, draining value without explanation.

The turning point came during a conversation with her financial advisor.

They reviewed her portfolio performance, retirement projections, and savings rate. Everything looked solid. Then Priya asked a simple question: "How much will I pay in taxes over my lifetime?"

The advisor paused.

There was no clear answer.

That night, Priya went home unsettled. She realized she had optimized everything except the one cost that touched every part of her financial life. Taxes were not just a line item—they were a shadow following every decision.

A few weeks later, a colleague mentioned an AI-powered financial and tax planning system that "connects everything together." Priya was skeptical. She had tools already. What she didn't have was clarity. Still, she decided to try.

The system began by building a complete financial model. Income history. Investment accounts. Retirement contributions. Tax filings. Everything was connected. When the dashboard appeared, Priya felt as though she was looking at her financial life from above for the first time.

Then she saw the projection.

Not just next year. Not just retirement. A lifetime view.

The system showed how her current decisions would play out over decades—how much she would earn, how much she would invest, how much would grow, and how much would be lost to taxes along the way. The number was staggering. Taxes represented one of the largest expenses she would ever incur, yet it was the least planned for.

What surprised Priya most was how small changes made a difference.

The AI simulated adjustments—slightly different retirement contributions, a reallocation of investments, timing of asset sales, strategic use of tax-advantaged accounts. Each change altered the long-term picture. Some increased short-term taxes but reduced lifetime burden. Others did the opposite. The system explained each trade-off clearly, without judgment.

For the first time, Priya understood that financial planning was not about maximizing one number—it was about aligning many over time.

As months passed, Priya began using the system as a guide rather than a crutch. Before making major decisions, she ran scenarios. Before increasing investments, she checked tax implications. Before helping family financially, she considered timing and structure. Taxes were no longer an afterthought—they were part of the conversation.

Years later, Priya reflected on how much had changed.

She was not working harder. She was not earning dramatically more. Yet her financial position felt stronger, more intentional, more resilient. The sense of leakage was gone. In its place was alignment.

One evening, reviewing her updated projections, Priya smiled.

The long view no longer felt intimidating.

It felt clear.

And for the first time, she knew exactly where her money was going—not just this year, but for the rest of her life.

Chapter 10

The Future of AI-Powered Personal Taxes and the End of Tax Anxiety

The future of personal taxation will not be defined by new forms, longer instructions, or more complex rules. It will be defined by intelligence. As artificial intelligence becomes embedded into financial systems, tax preparation will evolve from an annual event into a continuous, automated, and largely invisible process. The traditional concept of "doing taxes" will fade, replaced by systems that calculate, adjust, and file on your behalf in real time. This transformation is not speculative—it is already underway.

Governments around the world are digitizing tax administration at an unprecedented pace. Payroll data, banking activity, investment transactions, and platform income are increasingly reported automatically. The IRS already receives vast amounts of third-party data before most taxpayers ever open tax software. AI bridges the final gap by reconciling that data proactively, ensuring that what you file aligns perfectly with what institutions report. In the future, discrepancies will be the exception rather than the norm. One of the most significant shifts will be the rise of automated filing. Instead of assembling returns manually, taxpayers will receive pre-calculated filings generated by AI systems that already know their income, expenses, deductions, and credits. The role of the taxpayer will shift from data entry to review and approval. Filing will become a confirmation rather than a construction process. This will dramatically reduce errors, audits, and compliance costs across the system.

AI will also transform the relationship between taxpayers and tax authorities. Today, communication is reactive—letters arrive months later, requesting clarification or payment. In the AI-powered future, communication will be proactive. Systems will notify taxpayers of issues as they arise, recommend adjustments, and even negotiate resolution paths automatically. Compliance will feel less like enforcement and more like alignment.

Another major evolution will be personalized tax optimization at scale. AI systems will continuously analyze individual financial behavior, identifying opportunities to reduce taxes legally and strategically. These recommendations will be contextual, timing-aware, and tailored to life events. Instead of generic advice, taxpayers will receive guidance that reflects their unique situation. Taxes will become a design parameter rather than a penalty. AI will also play a central role in democratizing tax expertise. Historically, advanced tax strategies were available only to the wealthy, who could afford specialized advisors. AI levels the playing field by embedding sophisticated analysis into accessible platforms. This shift has profound implications for wealth equality, entrepreneurship, and economic mobility. When individuals can optimize taxes effectively, they retain more capital to invest, save, and grow.

As these systems mature, tax anxiety will diminish. Fear thrives in uncertainty. AI replaces uncertainty with visibility, predictability, and control. When taxpayers can see their tax position forming in real time, surprises disappear. When compliance is continuous, mistakes become rare. When planning is integrated, confidence replaces stress.

The future of taxes is not about avoiding responsibility—it is about removing unnecessary friction. AI does not change the obligation to pay taxes, but it changes how that obligation is met. It transforms a historically painful process into a managed system that operates quietly in the background of daily life.

Ultimately, the end of tax anxiety will not come from simpler laws, but from smarter systems. Artificial intelligence is that system. It represents the final evolution of personal taxation—from manual reporting to automated intelligence. Those who embrace it will not just file better returns. They will live with greater financial clarity, stability, and peace of mind.

"The Year Taxes Disappeared"

For as long as he could remember, Thomas measured the years by deadlines.

There was the end of the fiscal year. The rush of January forms. The quiet dread of March. And then April—always April—when everything came due at once. No matter how organized he tried to be, tax season felt like a reckoning. It interrupted routines, strained relationships, and cast a shadow over moments that should have felt celebratory.

Thomas was not careless. He was methodical by nature, a planner who tracked goals and maintained spreadsheets. Yet taxes never felt manageable. They felt external—something imposed rather than understood. Each year brought the same cycle of gathering, worrying, second-guessing, and hoping.

Then, without fanfare, things began to change.

It started when Thomas switched to a fully AI-driven tax platform, mostly out of curiosity. He expected incremental improvement. Maybe fewer forms. Maybe clearer explanations. What he did not expect was silence.

Weeks passed after he connected his accounts. Then months. No alerts. No frantic reminders. No piles of paperwork forming on his desk. The system worked quietly, pulling data, categorizing transactions, tracking deductions, and projecting outcomes without asking for constant attention.

At first, the absence of stress made Thomas uneasy.

He checked the dashboard often, half expecting something to be wrong. Instead, he saw a simple projection that updated gently as his life unfolded. Income rose and fell. Expenses appeared and were categorized. Investments moved. The tax position adjusted smoothly in the background, like a thermostat maintaining balance.

When a bonus arrived mid-year, Thomas braced instinctively. Old habits told him this would cause trouble later. Instead, the system updated his forecast, explained the impact, and suggested a minor adjustment. No panic. No confusion. Just clarity.

As the year progressed, Thomas noticed something subtle but profound: he stopped thinking about taxes altogether.

Not because he was ignoring them—but because they were handled.

There was no moment of dread when opening mail. No nights spent hunting for receipts. No frantic searches through old accounts. The system remembered everything. It anticipated what mattered and ignored what didn't. Taxes became background noise instead of a recurring crisis.

April arrived quietly.

Thomas realized it only because a notification appeared on his phone: *Your return is ready for review.* He opened it with curiosity rather than fear. The numbers matched what he had seen all year. No surprises. No shocks. Just confirmation.

He approved the filing in minutes.

That evening, Thomas reflected on how different this April felt. There was no relief because there had been no stress to escape. No celebration because nothing painful had occurred. Taxes had simply... happened.

Weeks later, a friend mentioned dreading tax season. Thomas listened, surprised by how distant the feeling seemed. He tried to remember the anxiety, the sleepless nights, the tightness in his chest when April approached. It felt like recalling a bad habit he had finally broken.

The following year was the same. And the year after that.

Taxes no longer marked time in Thomas's life. They no longer dictated emotional seasons or interrupted momentum. They became part of the infrastructure of his finances—automatic, reliable, and unremarkable.

One afternoon, while reviewing his long-term projections, Thomas smiled.

The future no longer felt like a series of deadlines.

It felt open. And for the first time in his adult life, taxes were no longer something he endured.

They were simply gone.

Final Thoughts

The End of Guesswork and the Beginning of Intelligent Control

For generations, personal taxes have been treated as an unavoidable burden—something endured rather than understood. People learned to fear tax season, to hope they had done enough, and to accept that confusion was simply part of the process. This mindset was never inevitable. It was the result of outdated systems forcing human beings to manage complexity that exceeded human capacity. Artificial intelligence changes that equation permanently.

Throughout this book, you have seen how AI transforms every stage of personal tax preparation. It does not simply automate what humans already do poorly; it redefines the entire process. Income is no longer something you reconstruct after the fact—it is tracked, understood, and classified in real time. Expenses are no longer lost or guessed—they are captured, documented, and optimized continuously. Errors are no longer discovered months later—they are prevented before filing ever occurs. Taxes stop being reactive and become proactive.

The most important shift is not technological—it is psychological. When people understand their tax position as it forms, fear dissolves. When uncertainty disappears, avoidance disappears with it. AI gives taxpayers visibility, and visibility creates control. That control extends beyond filing into planning, forecasting, investing, and long-term decision-making. Taxes become part of the financial architecture rather than a disruptive force.

This matters because taxes are one of the largest financial forces in a person's life. Over decades, small inefficiencies compound into massive losses. Missed deductions, poor timing, misclassified income, and reactive decisions quietly drain wealth year after year. AI interrupts that erosion. It replaces approximation with precision and replaces anxiety with clarity. It ensures that what you owe is accurate, defensible, and optimized—nothing more and nothing less.

Equally important is access. Advanced tax strategies were once reserved for corporations and high-net-worth individuals who could afford teams of advisors. AI democratizes that intelligence. It embeds sophisticated analysis into systems that ordinary taxpayers can use effortlessly. This leveling of the playing field has profound implications. When individuals keep more of what they earn legally and confidently, they gain capital to invest, build, and grow. Economic mobility accelerates. Financial literacy becomes experiential rather than theoretical. As governments adopt AI for enforcement, alignment becomes essential. Filing with intelligence is no longer optional—it is protective. AI-driven tax preparation ensures that your data matches what institutions report, that your records are complete, and that your compliance profile remains clean. In this environment, accuracy is not just beneficial; it is strategic.

Looking forward, the concept of "doing taxes" will continue to fade. Automated reporting, real-time reconciliation, and AI-driven filing will make manual preparation obsolete. Taxpayers will move from assembling returns to reviewing outcomes. Compliance will become continuous, and tax anxiety will become a relic of the past.

This book is not about avoiding taxes. It is about removing unnecessary friction, waste, and fear from a system that touches every financial decision you make. Artificial intelligence does not change your obligations—but it changes your experience. It transforms taxation from a yearly disruption into a quiet, intelligent system that works in the background of your life.

If there is one message to take forward, it is this: clarity is power. When you understand how your money flows, how your taxes are calculated, and how decisions affect outcomes, you are no longer at the mercy of the system. You are operating within it—confidently, legally, and intelligently.

The era of guesswork is over. The era of AI-powered personal taxes has begun.

www.ingramcontent.com/pod-product-compliance
Ingram Content Group UK Ltd.
Pitfield, Milton Keynes, MK11 3LW, UK
UKHW020156290926
15471UKWH00005B/906

9 798295 585982